D1421089

BARLEY HALL

A DAY IN A MEDIEVAL Town House

Charles Kightly

WAYLAND

Titles in the Series

Fishbourne – A Day in a Roman Palace
Barley Hall – A Day in a Medieval Town House

Series Editor: Cathy Baxter
Series Designer: Loraine Hayes
Book Designer: Jean Wheeler
Artist: Chris Forsey

First Published in 1997 by Wayland (Publishers) Ltd
61 Western Road, Hove, East Sussex, BN3 1JD, England

British Library Cataloging in Publication Data
Kightly, Charles
Barley Hall – A Day in a Medieval Town House.
(What Life Was Like Series)
I. Title II. Series
942.044

HARDBACK ISBN 0 7502 1608 5

Typeset by Jean Wheeler
Colour reproduction by Page Turn, Hove, East Sussex
Printed and bound in Italy by G. Canale & CSpA, Turin

Picture acknowledgements:
Archiv für Kunst und Geschichte 20; Bibliothèque Royale, Albert I, Brussels 23 (bottom); The Bridgeman Art Library, London 6, 14 (bottom); The British Library 7 (both), 11, 12, 13, 16, 18 (bottom); English Heritage 30–31 (all); E.T. Archive 29; Glasgow Museum and Art Gallery 15; National Gallery of Victoria, Melbourne, Australia 17 (top), 19; Erica Twyman 27; York Archaeological Trust 2–3, 4, 10, 14 (top), 17 (bottom), 18 (top), 21 (both), 22 (both), 26 (both); Yorkshire Museum 23.

Contents

Introduction

William Snawsell and his family live in Barley Hall, a fine house near the centre of the great city of York, one of the biggest towns in medieval England. York has a famous cathedral (the Minster), a castle, and many churches and monasteries. Its houses, shops and busy market places are all crowded together within a strong city wall.

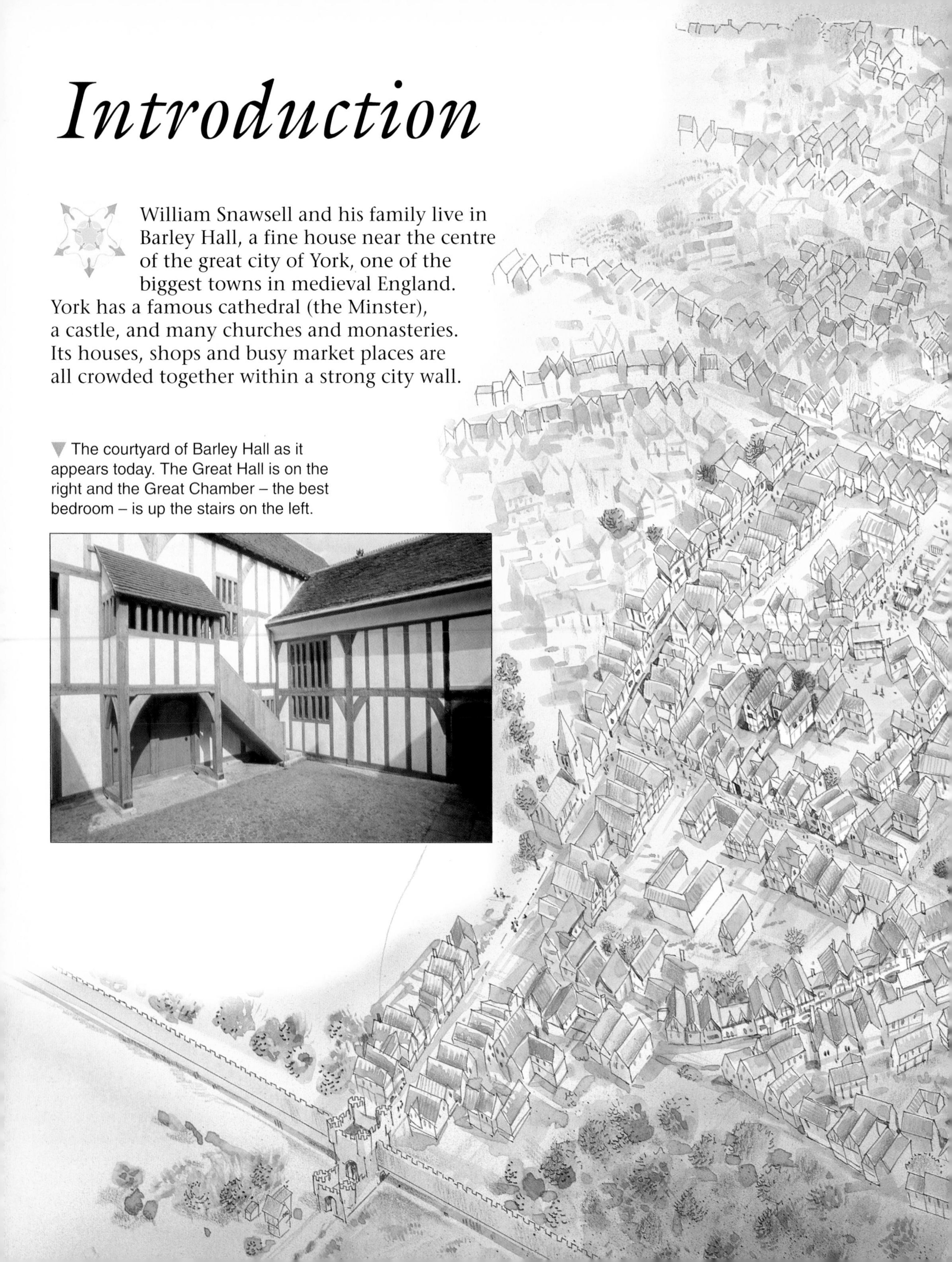

▼ The courtyard of Barley Hall as it appears today. The Great Hall is on the right and the Great Chamber – the best bedroom – is up the stairs on the left.

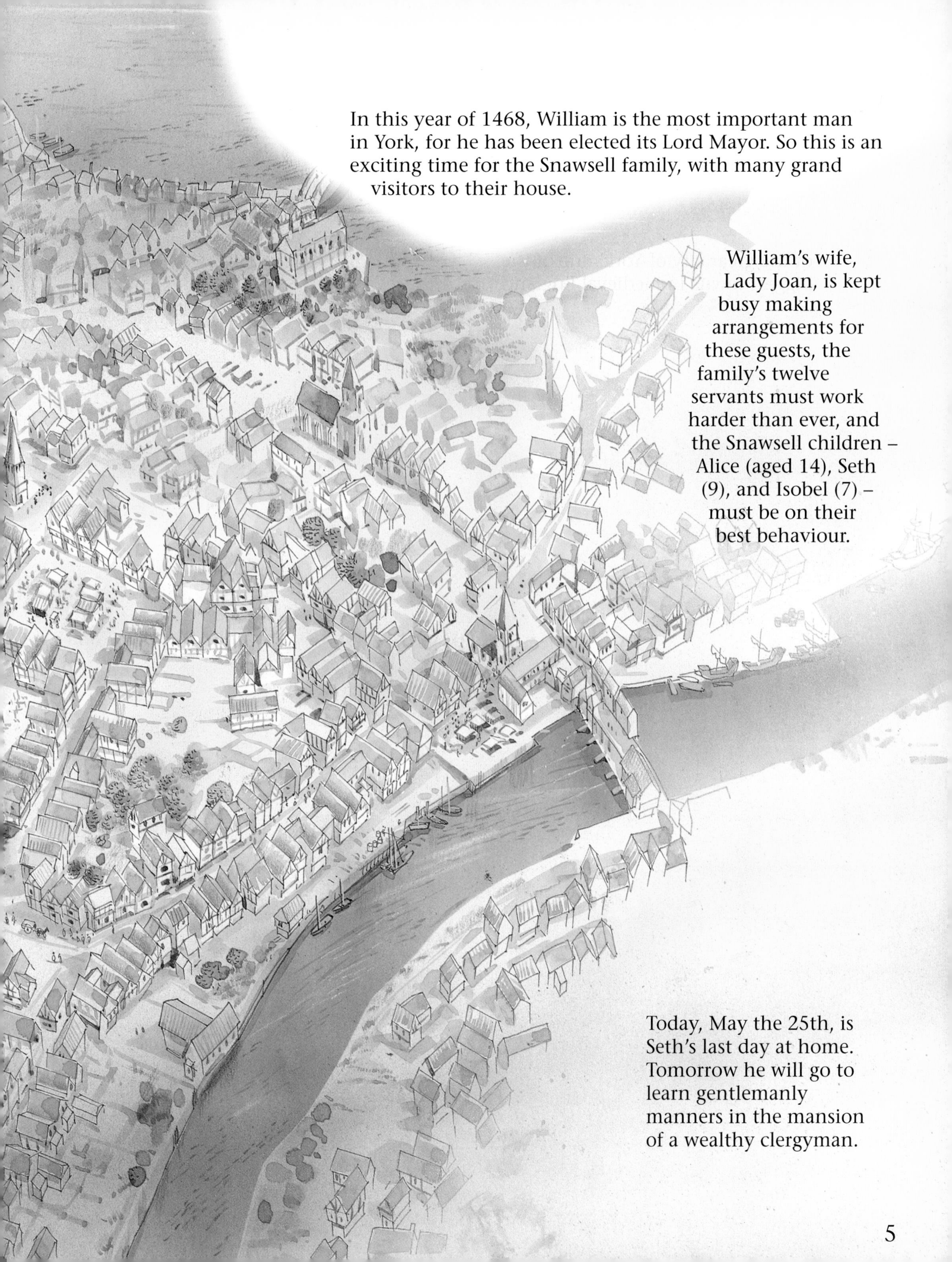

In this year of 1468, William is the most important man in York, for he has been elected its Lord Mayor. So this is an exciting time for the Snawsell family, with many grand visitors to their house.

William's wife, Lady Joan, is kept busy making arrangements for these guests, the family's twelve servants must work harder than ever, and the Snawsell children – Alice (aged 14), Seth (9), and Isobel (7) – must be on their best behaviour.

Today, May the 25th, is Seth's last day at home. Tomorrow he will go to learn gentlemanly manners in the mansion of a wealthy clergyman.

▲ A fifteenth century goldsmith's shop, with customers buying jewels. The cupboard displays gold and silver tableware, buckles and rings.

Seth is worried about beginning a new life in strange surroundings, among the sons of knights and squires. He had hoped to become a goldsmith and jeweller like his father, and one day take over the family shop near York Minster.

Seth will miss the comforting sound of hammering from the workshop behind Barley Hall, where his father's craftsmen beat silver and gold into cups and plates for customers. This trade has made the Snawsells very prosperous, and they want Seth to do even better. Perhaps he will become a country landowner like his mother's relations.

Nearly all their neighbours in Stonegate – York's grandest street – also produce expensive things for wealthy buyers, or to beautify cathedrals and churches. The shops of goldsmiths, embroiderers, painters and stained-glass makers line the street, and their owners usually live in the rooms above. Only the most prosperous merchants (like the Snawsells of Barley Hall) have houses set back from the noisy road.

▲ All medieval tableware was handmade. These craftsmen are using hammers to shape gold into cups and candlesticks.

Fact Box

There were no banks in medieval England, so rich people converted their money into gold plate and jewellery. This could be sold in hard times, and meanwhile showed off its owner's wealth and importance.

Even the tiniest chippings from goldsmiths' workshops were valuable. Craftsmen wore sheepskin aprons to catch the gold-dust: old aprons were burnt to melt out the precious metal.

▼ A medieval street, with open-fronted shops at ground level, and living rooms above. Most houses are of timber, like Barley Hall.

Like most York houses, Barley Hall has a framework of massive oak timbers, fastened together by wooden pegs. In between are panels of plastered-over brick, made in the city's brickworks along with the clay roof tiles.

The tallest wing of the house contains bed-chambers above ground floor storerooms. William and Joan sleep in the 'Great Chamber', with its blue cloth wall-hangings. This is also the family's sitting room, with its own entrance via the courtyard and stairway.

Fact Box

Medieval houses were mainly lit by candles. The best were made of sweet-smelling, long-burning beeswax. Cheaper but smellier candles were made of tallow (animal fat) or of hollowed-out rushes soaked in fat (rushlights). But most people went to bed soon after sundown.

The Great Hall, with its chequered tile floor, is the biggest room in the house. Family and guests eat at the 'high table' across its top end. At the other end is the main entrance passage, leading to the kitchen, buttery and pantry.

Above these is the parlour, with its striped hangings. This is William's 'office', where he meets important visitors and customers.

The Kitchen

It is 3.30 a.m. when Walter the scullion wakes in the corner of the kitchen. The fleas have been biting him again – he really must change the straw in his mattress. The Minster bell is already ringing for the first service of the day, though it is not yet fully light. He had better get up and stoke the kitchen fires, before Peter the cook starts to shout at him.

Fact Box

Every job in a medieval house was done by hand, without electricity, gas or labour-saving machines. So servants were employed – mostly men and boys.

Some great lords kept hundreds of them. Servants began work young, sometimes at seven years old. They usually lived with their employer, who paid them mainly in food and clothing.

A bronze cauldron, used for boiling food, with a hook to hang it over the fire.

It is going to be a busy day for ten-year-old Walter, the lowest ranking and – he thinks – the hardest working of the twelve Barley Hall servants. With special guests coming to dinner and supper, there will be mountains of meat and vegetables to chop. These will be boiled in bronze cauldrons hung over the fire. Then there will be a whole piglet to roast on a spit above the flames. Walter must turn the spit slowly – however hot he gets – so that the meat cooks evenly.

Lady Joan will probably visit the kitchen, making the cook even more bad-tempered than usual. She is a kind mistress, but inclined to fuss and interfere, especially now that William is Lord Mayor.

▲ A medieval lady visits her kitchen. One cook chops meat, the other holds a frying pan over the fire.

Dawn

It is 4 a.m. and fully light, but Lord Mayor William Snawsell is still asleep in his big curtained and canopied bed in the Great Chamber. His personal servant, Robert Symson the chamberlain, quietly creeps in and opens the window shutters, then draws back the bed curtain and wishes his master 'Good morrow'.

▼ Fifteenth century ladies in a bedchamber, its walls lined with colourful hangings. At night the shutters are closed, and curtains are drawn around the bed.

He holds out a clean shirt (like everyone else, William wears only a nightcap in bed) and politely looks away as William gets up to use his 'stool of ease' or portable lavatory. Someone will empty it down the privy later. After saying his morning prayer, William sits in a chair while Robert combs his long hair and reports a quiet night in the city.

Next William puts on his hosen, the long cloth stockings which cover his thighs, legs and feet. Robert helps him lace them to his pourpoint, a close-fitting jerkin. Which gown should he wear over it today? Since an official visitor is expected, it had better be his long, scarlet mayor's robe.

▲ A gentleman getting dressed. The kneeling servant hands him his hosen.

In the Lesser Chamber next door, Lady Joan is giving her children a reading lesson. Isobel keeps fidgeting. Her mother reminds her that even the Virgin Mary had to learn to read. Isobel remembers the stained-glass window in the church, showing the Virgin being taught by her own mother Saint Anne. Seth tries harder – his new master will expect him to write as well as read.

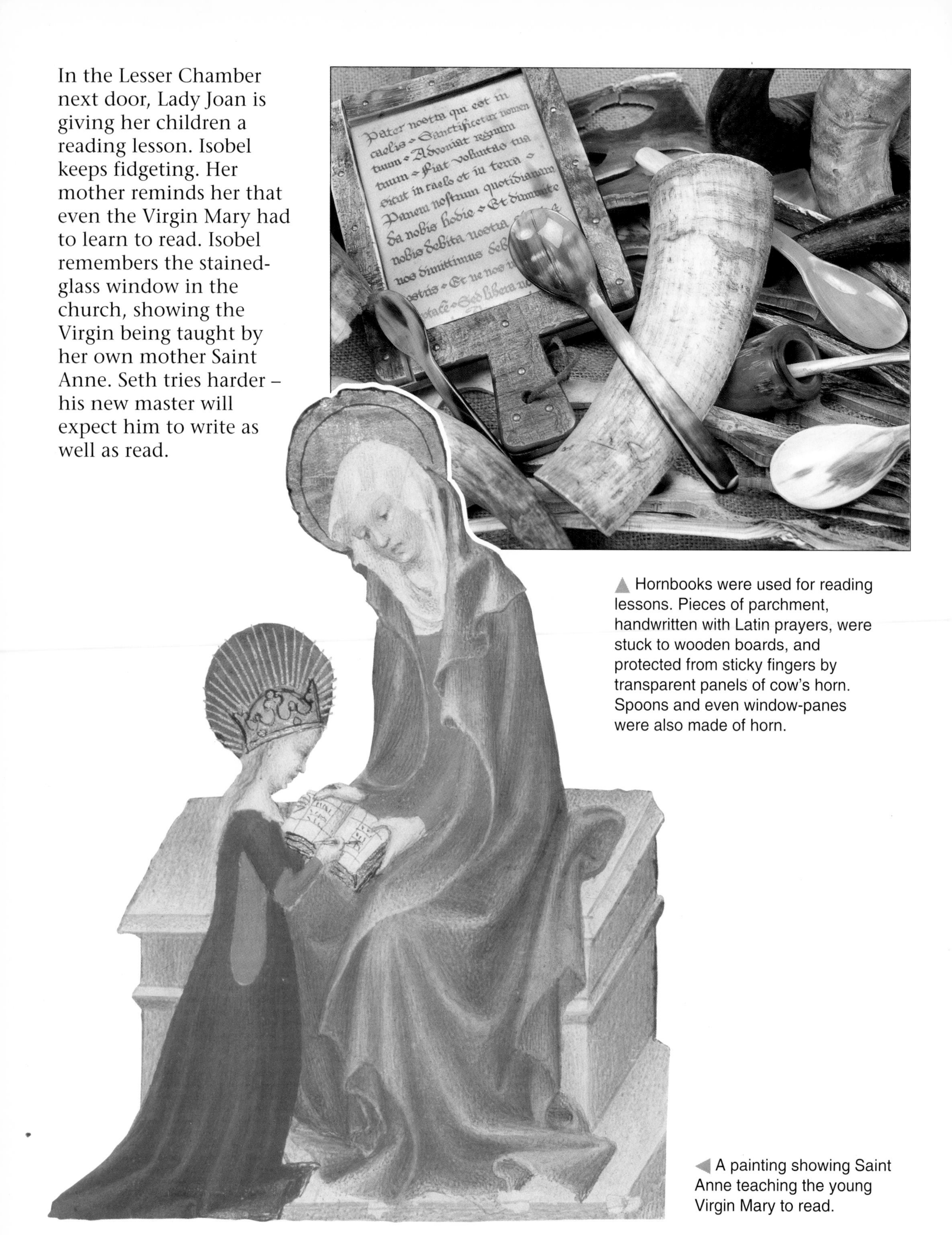

▲ Hornbooks were used for reading lessons. Pieces of parchment, handwritten with Latin prayers, were stuck to wooden boards, and protected from sticky fingers by transparent panels of cow's horn. Spoons and even window-panes were also made of horn.

◀ A painting showing Saint Anne teaching the young Virgin Mary to read.

Fourteen-year-old Alice tries not to envy her brother. Seth is only moving across the city, but she must go to faraway London when she marries John Stocker. She has only met John once, at their engagement ceremony: he seemed a nice boy, though rather nervous, and she is sure her parents have chosen her a good husband.

All the same, Alice will say a prayer in front of her mother's holy image of Christ and the saints, begging that John's family will be kind to her. Seth also glances at the alabaster carving in its brightly painted box. If he prays hard, perhaps he won't drop a plate when he serves his new master at supper this evening.

Fact Box

Everyone in medieval England believed in God and the saints. They went to church not only on Sundays but also on many other holy days. There were over a hundred of these holidays each year, when no one was supposed to work.

▼ A carving of Christ's head surrounded by saints. Wealthy medieval families treasured images like this in their houses.

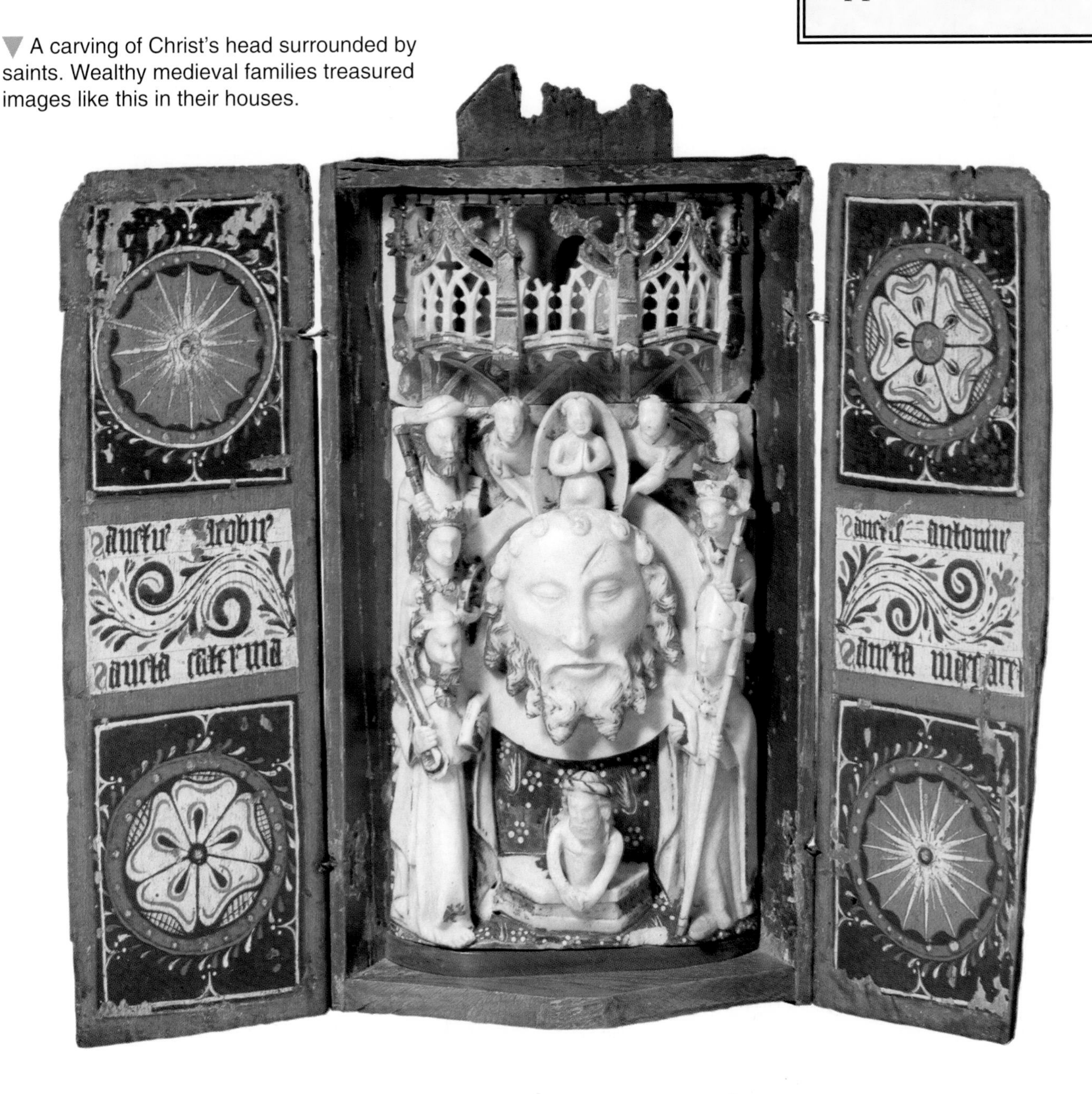

Mid morning

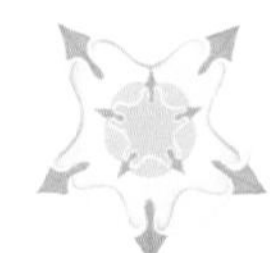

It is 10 a.m. and Matilda the laundress arrives in the storeroom with a bundle of clean linen bed sheets and tablecloths. She has soaked them in hot water, scrubbed and beaten them to pound out the dirt, and rinsed them in the river. After drying them on a line, she stretches them out on the grass and then folds them carefully. It is very hard work.

▼ This sixteenth-century manuscript shows laundresses washing linen, while a fire heats water in the cauldron.

▲ A servant returns with wooden buckets of water from the local well.

Fact Box

Linen – used instead of cotton for sheets, tablecloths, shirts and other 'whites' – is made from the stems of the flax plant. Its quality varied from rough 'servants' linen' to almost transparent 'cobweb lawn'.

Matilda is not pleased to find more dirty washing at Barley Hall. Lady Joan needs more clean shirts for Seth, and clean table napkins for unexpected guests – they will have to be washed at once. So old Martin the storeman goes off grumbling to fill his buckets at the well in Syke Alley, the nearest well to Barley Hall.

At least the well water is cleaner than river water, thinks Matilda as she starts to scrub. The townspeople use their river as a rubbish dump, and even the filthy waste from the butcher's shops is tipped into it.

▶ Medieval buckets were made of wooden staves, hooped with iron. If the wood was allowed to dry out and shrink, they would leak.

▲ The buttery at Barley Hall. The wooden barrels contain wine or ale, which is poured into the pottery jugs.

In the buttery at the other end of the house, Roger Banes the butler is checking his barrels. If barrels let in air, the wine they contain will be spoilt, and Master Snawsell will be angry when Roger pours a bowl for him to taste. Wine is expensive, because it must be brought by ship from France, or even Italy or Greece. Only the best wine will do for the Lord Mayor and his guests, but most of the household (including the children) drink home-brewed ale.

◄ Medieval coopers (barrel-makers) making hoops to hold barrels together, and hammering them onto a new barrel.

Meanwhile, in the pantry, Harry the bread-man is cutting trenchers – square slices from a hard, four-day-old loaf. These will be used instead of plates, with food ladled onto them. Harry hopes he has enough manchets, the fresh round rolls people use to soak up gravy or soup from their bowls.

Dinner is now nearly ready, and for once Peter the cook is in a good mood. The main dishes today are piglet and goose, but he has also managed to buy a dozen larks in the market, and baked them in a pie. That should impress the master's grand guest.

▼ A fifteenth-century feast scene, showing round manchet rolls and rectangular boards for trenchers. The butler pours drink into huge pottery jugs.

Fact Box

Medieval people ate many foods that are unusual today. Meats included deer, pork, lamb and chicken.

On Fridays, and for forty days before Easter, fish (including dolphins and whales) was eaten instead of meat. Potatoes were unknown.

Midday

It is twelve noon, and all the household gather in the Great Hall for the main meal of the day. The servants sit on benches at tables along the sides of the room, but the Snawsell family eat in state at the high table on its raised platform.

The best diamond-pattern tablecloth has been laid in honour of their guest, Sir Thomas Burgh. He has come on a mysterious mission from the King, and Isobel tries hard not to stare at him.

▼ A medieval meal. Honoured guests sit under a canopy at the high table, while trumpeters play in the gallery. Silver plates are displayed on the carved sideboard.

Fact Box

Table forks were unknown in medieval England. Everyone carried a sharp knife to cut up their food, and ate with their fingers. Greasy fingers were wiped on bread rolls or, in wealthier families, washed in bowls of scented water brought round by servants.

When the parish priest has said grace, William signals Peter the cook and Robert Symson to begin serving dinner. All the dishes – including meats, vegetable pottage or stew, and spiced stewed fruit – are brought in at the same time, so that people can pick and mix as they like.

Naturally the high table is served first, and the special lark pie is set before Sir Thomas. Seth ladles some pottage into his bowl with a silver spoon. Then, after glancing at his father for permission, he cuts off a piece of piglet to put on his trencher. Like everyone else, he uses his own private knife to cut up his meat, but eats it with his fingers.

◀ Medieval eating knives were sharp. Putting them in your mouth was dangerous as well as rude. The spoon is made of pewter.

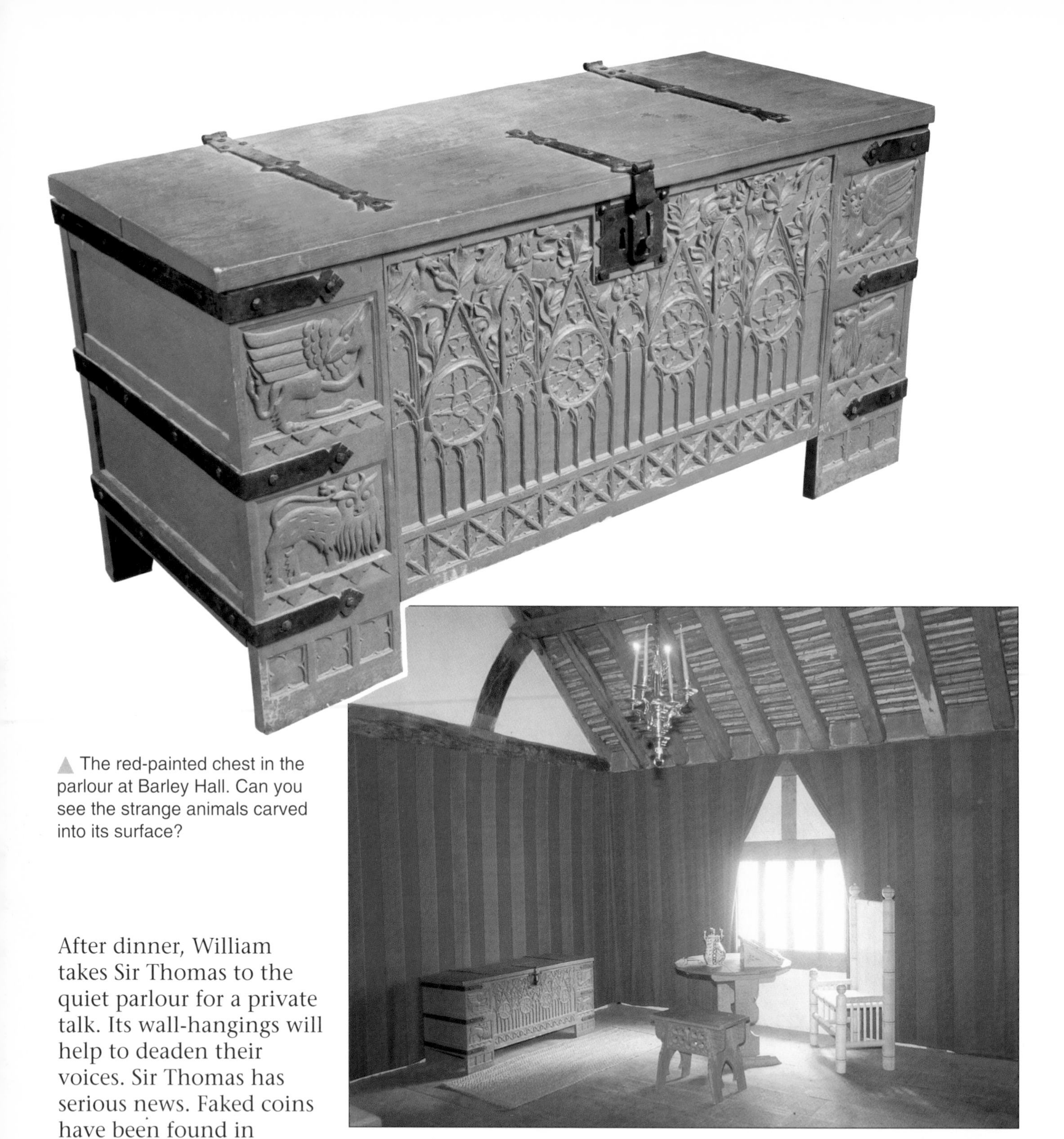

▲ The red-painted chest in the parlour at Barley Hall. Can you see the strange animals carved into its surface?

▲ The parlour at Barley Hall, with its striped-cloth wall hangings and brass chandelier. Hangings brightened medieval rooms and kept out draughts.

After dinner, William takes Sir Thomas to the quiet parlour for a private talk. Its wall-hangings will help to deaden their voices. Sir Thomas has serious news. Faked coins have been found in London. They are copies of those produced at the York Mint, but made of silvered brass instead of real silver. Someone must have stolen one of the die-stamps on which coins are hammered out. This affects William directly, because – as well as being Lord Mayor – he is Master of the York Mint. The criminal must be caught and hanged. William hopes it is not one of his own craftsmen.

Sir Thomas asks for a list of workers in the mint, and William unlocks the 'red chest'. The chest is a family treasure, left to William by his grandmother. He takes out a sheet of paper, then sits down to copy the list, first using his penknife to cut himself a new goose-feather pen. Dipping his pen in the horn inkwell, he begins writing. When he has finished, he dries the ink with fine sand, rolls up the parchment, and seals the roll with wax stamped with his own seal. Now nobody will be able to open it without Sir Thomas's knowledge.

◀ A silver penny of King Richard III, made at the York Mint.

▼ Writing at a desk, using a penknife and quill pen.

The Great Hall

It is 8 p.m. and normally the Barley Hall household would be preparing for bed. But this is a special evening, because Seth's new master, Canon John Guisborough, has come to supper in the Great Hall. So has his father's friend, Thomas Uscliffe, the chapman, or travelling salesman.

For once, Seth is not interested in the new kind of scales the chapman demonstrates. He is too busy serving Canon Guisborough, a big man in a mulberry-coloured gown, who wears a gold chain round his neck bought from Seth's father. A little cap covers the shaven patch (or tonsure) on his head which shows he is a clergyman. But John is no ordinary parish priest. He is one of the canons who rule York Minster, and is one of the richest and most powerful men in the city.

Since it is late, the meal is a simple one: just cold roast swan, sweet wafer biscuits and fruit. When it is over, Seth brings a bowl of scented water to wash the guests' hands, and dries them with a clean towel.

▶ A bowl for spiced wine with two stags swimming in it. Joke bowls like this were popular in medieval York.

▲ A cushion embroidered with a parrot, the badge of Seth's mother's family.

▲ The Great Hall at Barley Hall, with its high table and brightly tiled floor. The wall hangings are painted with white roses.

Smiling at Seth, the Canon hopes he will make friends among the other boys being educated in his mansion. Seth has served so well tonight that the Canon has decided to begin the boy's training at once. Tomorrow evening he will wait on the Canon's noble guests at a great banquet, held to honour the feast of Christ's Ascension.

When the Canon has gone, Seth sits quietly with his parents. They remind him how exciting it will be to live in a grand mansion. Seth only thinks how much he will miss the familiar surroundings of Barley Hall. Reading his mind, his mother gives him a cushion embroidered with her family's badge, to remind him of home.

Evening

It is past nine p.m., but the long day is not yet over. Lady Joan insists that everybody must have a bath, to be clean for tomorrow's Ascension Day Holy day. So gallons of water must be heated in cauldrons over the kitchen fire, and poured into big wooden tubs. Poor Walter, of course, is the last to climb into the servants' tub in the storeroom. The water is already very dirty by then.

The Snawsell family bathe more privately in the Great Chamber. Their tub is lined with linen cloths to protect them against splinters and contains a stool to sit on. As a treat, Seth is allowed in first, then the girls, then Lady Joan, then William. Most of the water has been splashed out by then, so Robert and Harry pour in more.

▶ A couple and their dog sleep in a curtained bed. They wear nightcaps to keep their heads warm.

As soon as they have dried themselves, the Snawsell family go straight to bed. Everyone must be up for the early church service tomorrow, before Seth sets off from Barley Hall for his new life.

Nearly all the people in this story really existed, and lived in or near Barley Hall. Alice did marry John Stocker and their descendants now live in Oxford. Isobel stayed in York and married a lawyer.

After several years in Canon Guisborough's household, Seth did eventually become a country landowner. Like his father William, he lived to be a very old man: he married twice, and had twenty-two children.

Many centuries later, one of his descendants (also called Seth) emigrated to Australia. Lady Joan's family badge really was a green parrot: you can see it carved on her relations' tombs in Sheriff Hutton church, near York.

Fact Box

Very few people slept in privacy. Poorer families often shared a single large bed, and travellers at inns would expect to share beds with several strangers. Even wealthy people often had a servant sleeping in the corner of their bedroom, in case they needed anything.

Places to visit

Barley Hall, restored by the York Archaeological Trust, stands in Coffee Yard, an alleyway off Stonegate in the centre of York. The rooms and objects photographed in this book can be seen there. For opening times, ring the York Archaeological Trust on 01904 643211.

Many of the places the Snawsells would have known, including York Minster, the Guildhall, where the medieval council met, and the Merchant Adventurers' Hall, can also be visited in York.

Medieval houses and places of interest in other parts of Britain include the following:

Aydon 'Castle', Corbridge, Northumberland.

Stokesay 'Castle', near Ludlow, Shropshire.

Tudor Merchant's House, Tenby, Dyfed.

Markenfield Hall, near
Ripon, North Yorkshire.
Gainsborough Old Hall,
Gainsborough,
Lincolnshire.
Longthorpe Tower,
Peterborough.
Tretower Court,
Powys.
The Mediaeval
Merchant's House,
Southampton.

Glossary

alabaster A soft stone, easily carved and painted. Used mainly for religious images and statues.

buttery A room where drink was stored, usually in 'butts' (or barrels). The butler, the man in charge of drink, worked there.

cauldrons Large pots of bronze or iron, used for boiling food or water.

chamberlain A personal servant, who worked in his employer's private chamber.

pantry A room for storing and preparing food, especially bread ('pain' in French).

parchment Scraped and prepared sheets of sheepskin, used instead of paper for medieval books and letters.

parlour Literally, a room where people talk (from the French 'parler', to speak).

privy A lavatory, often just a seat above a hole in the ground or (if upstairs) over a shaft leading to a hole.

spit A prong on which meat is roasted.

scullion A servant who did the messiest jobs in the kitchen.

stained glass Pieces of coloured glass, used to make up pictures in church windows. Fine details were painted on the surface of the glass.

Index